# *Calling In the Dawn*

# *Calling In the Dawn*

## Shaping Our Future through Authentic Dialogue

by

### Kathleen Macferran

STRENGTH OF CONNECTION
www.StrengthofConnection.com

Text by Kathleen Macferran
Designed by Kenneth Schrag
Photo credits: Kathleen Macferran

Calling in the Dawn/Kathleen Macferran- 1st ed.
Published 3/1/2024
Publisher: Strength of Connection
Library of Congress Control Number: 2024903209
Paperback ISBN 978-1-962606-08-0
eBook ISBN 978-1-962606-18-9

Published in Seattle, WA USA

*This book is dedicated to:*

*those who dare to listen deeply*
*and those who dare to speak from the heart.*
*You are my hope.*

*those who carry out acts of kindness*
*- no matter how big or small.*
*You are my light.*

*and those who tirelessly do the sacred work*
*to create a better world for our children.*
*You are my heroes.*

# Table of Contents

# Letter to My Readers

I believe in the power of authentic dialogue. I believe it is foundational to every aspect of our lives. People talk, things happen. I also believe the quality of our dialogues directly correlates to the quality of our lives. Conversations precede our choices to dehumanize and destroy each other, or to create spaces where we all thrive.

Each of us are co-creators of and responsible for our conversations. How we talk and how we listen are choices we each make again and again. Individual choice is not isolated choice, however. Our access to inner choice and the external options available to us in any moment are influenced by larger social patterns and systems.

I cannot think of another area of investment that could make a more beneficial change for this world than individuals, communities and organizations becoming more skillful in authentic dialogue. Dialogue is a user-friendly, intuitive, free and regenerative resource. I strongly believe that if we can "up our game" in how we listen and talk, millions of lives, trillions of dollars, and thousands of species could be saved.

Given the amount of conversation in the world today then why are we not in better shape? Some of our conversations lead to war, environmental destruction, and inequitable distribution of resources. Some of our conversations lead to food production, medical care, and education for billions of people. What's the difference?

This book is an attempt to explore some answers to those questions. I'll speak to the essence of practices I've encountered in my journey as a certified trainer with the Center for Nonviolent Communication. I'll also offer bits of wisdom I've learned as an everyday global citizen who is trying to understand the inequities of our world. This book explores simple principles of each named topic, inviting readers to integrate those ideas with their own personal life learnings.

To be clear, this book is meant to be both practical and aspirational. It is born of ground and prayer, side by side. I invite each of us to concretely and courageously name what our hearts want, while acknowledging any despair and hopelessness that constrains our vision. I have tried to capture actual felt bodily experiences from multiple life perspectives (earth/ground), as well as name the world I passionately hope to help co-create (vision/prayer).

Many parts of this book are written in first person "I," inviting the reader to feel what it might be like if that experience were their own. This is an invitation to feel into what resonates with your own experience, imagine the felt sense of experiences different than your own, then reimagine what is possible if we bravely ask for nothing less than the moon.

So bring your whole self to the reading of this book. Logic and heart. All parts are not only welcome, but essential for constructing new creative possibilities for how we live.

This book opens with my vision of a future world that works for ALL, which I call "the dawn" because of the exquisite beauty and new possibilities each dawn brings. No matter the degree of darkness, the first light of each day promises transformation.

In Chapter 1: Inner Resources, I explore personal practices of peace and nonviolence as a way of being, as daily training and inquiry. I believe that each of us can make powerful choices that affect our own and others' well-being. Cultivating our inner resources is a responsible act of love.

In Chapter 2: Systemic Awareness, I define and explore vocabulary and contextual considerations to bring awareness to the influences of larger systems, patterns, and cultural norms on individual and group experiences that impact our ability for open, authentic dialogue.

In Chapter 3: Dialogue in Action, is where I explore authentic dialogue as a collective daily practice. I believe peace and nonviolence is cultivated in relationship, resonance, warmth, and honoring of our collective wisdom. Becoming skilled in dialogue, no matter how hard, is critical for our survival.

At the end of the book are discussion and/or journaling questions if you or your community would like to explore what this book means for you personally.

Let the inquiry begin…

Warmly,
Kathleen

# What is "the Dawn"?

*The exquisitely beautiful,*
*peaceful, loving world yet to be born*
*that is waiting for us on the horizon.*

*The emerging world that is*
*waiting for our hearts to break open*
*and bravely cross the threshold of living*
*from the sacred, fiery love that we truly are.*

*The world daring us to build*
*beyond the forms we have outgrown.*

*A world*
*where:*

*Everyone has an equitable place at the table.*

*All are celebrated*
*as vital in the interconnected web of life,*
*treated with dignity and honored for their gifts.*

*We root ourselves in trust, ground in love,*
*dissolve hate, and rise above violence.*

*We use our wings*
*to fly to our highest potential,*
*as well as to shelter each other from the cold winds.*

*Climbing out of poverty and war is sacred work,*
*community work, collaborative work.*

*Conflict is an opportunity*
*to tend to what we deeply care about*
*in life-affirming ways for all involved.*

*When bridges break between us, they are repaired,*
*fortified with community support*
*until they are sturdier and more resilient than before.*

*Possibility is no longer constrained*
*by limits of imagination,*
*but innovation and creativity*
*are the air we breath and waters we drink.*

*Love rides freely in the wind,*
*touching everything in its path.*

*The call for courage enlivens us*
*to claim radical inclusive love*
*and create beloved, thriving community*
*everywhere.*

# Why Call In the Dawn?

*Because life is sacred*
*and I want all of us to be able to relish*
*the magnificence of life and live it fully.*

*With my first breath in this world I inhaled air*
*tainted by inequity and the bitter acridness of war,*
*yet permeated with profound love and beauty.*

*Innocent and bewildered by the contrast,*
*my soul discovered its purpose:*
*"To live love in ways that benefit and serve all Beings."*

*Since then, my life has been a complex journey through fire*
*in the healing belly of the dragon seeking a place*
*where what is hurt is transformed by love.*

*I pray my final exhale will be clear,*
*giving back to the world unconditional love, joy, peace,*
*and gratitude for all that is beautiful.*

*But, there is work to do before that final breath.*
*I have so much to learn.*

*This book is my attempt to support*
*the collective cultivation of skills*
*to aid us in calling in the dawn.*

*Our survival urgently asks us to tend mindfully*
*to our interconnected web of relationships.*

*Love demands that we learn its ways or die.*

*Now is the time to learn to talk with one another,*
*to learn from one another.*

*Now is the time to heal relationships ruptured by violence,*
*destroyed by war, deadened by hate.*

*Now is the time to know the future of everything we value*
*hinges on our actions in this moment and the next.*

*Now is the time to raise our children*
*in the arms of trusting and loving relationship*
*so they may live with strong, undefended hearts*
*and soar beyond horizons we can't yet see.*

*I choose love and life in the form of this book.*
*It's my action to catalyze innovative possibilities,*
*a compassionate compass to point our way*
*to inner resilience, collective learning,*
*dynamic peace and an equitable world.*

*May it be a reminder*
*of the inevitability of love*
*if we but persist.*

13

## CHAPTER 1

# Inner Resources

❧

## How Can We Cultivate Inner Resources to Call In the Dawn?

*Practice.*

*Experiment boldly with nonviolence.*

*Learn from ancient and contemporary wisdom
how to talk with one another.*

*Be guided by the rhythms, cycles, seasons of the earth.
Sync the pacing of our hearts and heads
to the longings of the soul.*

*Repair harm, restore relationships,
find joy in contributing to one another.*

*When the night winds and discouragement come,
cup the flame of the heart to keep it safe,
slowly move it to shelter,
let our pace be guided by the flicker of the fire.*

*Feed the flame.
Burn.
Radiate heat and gratitude.*

*Learn to care for the fire inside and between each other.*
*Learn to care for our basic goodness.*
*Our teachers are everywhere, within and without.*

*Choose to be fire keepers of the dawning world.*

*Create conditions where life-affirming visions are fueled*
*and protected amidst the strong icy winds*
*of blame and polarization.*

*Act as if our life depends on cultivating*
*courageous equity and dynamic peace.*
*It does.*

*This alive, resilient, new world is waiting to come into form*
*through our daily choices and cultivated practices.*

*Self-reflect. Do inner work.*
*Heed the call of the horizon*
*Listen…Choose…Act…*

*These times call on us to do all we can,*
*to move toward the light together*
*and call in the dawn.*

*Carrying each other,*
*never giving up.*

# *Self-Connection*

*When I have lost my way,*
*dizzy from criticism, greed, and empty pursuits,*
*numb from high-speed chases to nowhere,*
*I close my eyes and wander the mysterious, wild inner woods*
*to find my way back to myself.*

*I arrive gently in the arms of my non-negotiable worth,*
*pulled by gravity into the center of my Being.*

*I align my bones to stand in my full integrity so I can move*
*in any direction with grace, speed and balance.*

*My eyes look to the horizon where my soul's purpose shines.*
*Diving into my heart I am transformed*
*by what deeply matters to me.*

*My breath reminds me to never give up*
*my power to choose and engage,*
*anchoring my unique path of integrity and heart*
*into my thoughts and actions.*

*My hands invite me to take full responsibility for my life.*
*My shoulders bear the freedom required to do so.*

*In the process of becoming,*
*I trust the emergence of my inner voice,*
*never surrendering my inner knowing,*
*always growing and expanding*
*my understanding of life.*

*My heart knows that radical self-love*
*is the foundation for collective liberation*
*so I wildly embrace my essential dignity,*
*understanding that my dignity is tied to yours.*

*I take time to be still and reflective.*
*I feel and embrace all that I feel.*
*I love what I love.*

*I am alert-*
*it may be time to break into blossom.*

# *Presence*

*Be*
*Here*
*Now*

*Be*
*the*
*Stillness*
*at*
*the*
*Heart*
*of*
*Silence*

*Be*
*Attentive*
*as*
*the*
*Heron*
*in*
*the*
*Moonlit*
*Lake*

*Be*
*With*
*What*
*Is*

*Be*
*Breath*

*Be*
*All*
*of*
*Who*
*I*
*Am*

*Be*
*Here*
*Now*

*Be*

# *Noticing*

*Mountain lions sniff earth and air*
*while Eagles scan the river for fish.*
*Worms sense light through their skin*
*while Bees chase ultraviolet color patterns to food.*
*In the dark, Snakes sense heat*
*while Bats maneuver through soundscapes.*
*Sandhill Cranes follow the earth's magnetic field home,*
*as Whales glean songs across a thousand miles.*
*All notice different parts of the world.*
*All perceptions real.*

*So it is with us.*
*We wander through realms of earth and spirit*
*following warmth, breath, light, sound and touch*
*to find each other.*

*Each seeing what we are trained to see.*
*Each sensing what we are taught*
*by our circumstances to sense.*
*All perceptions nuanced and sound.*

*I lift my face from the map and take in the territory.*
*Cedar fills my nostrils,*
*big leaf maple splashes red across my eyes,*
*the stirring of a frog catches my gaze.*
*Cool breeze caresses my arms as my feet feel soft ground.*
*Blood pumps life through my veins.*

*Honoring my body and my unique experience*
*I pause to simply be with what is.*

*I notice the story I spin from what I see, hear, sense*
*and the meaning it holds in my mind.*
*Distinguishing my internal filters and judgments*
*from what I actually observe*
*helps me trust what is happening*
*and choose my response wisely.*

*I pay attention to you, to the words, expressions*
*and ways you move through the world.*
*I watch without filters to ground in what is happening*
*rather than my thoughts about*
*what ought to happen.*

*I notice social behaviors and patterns*
*molding the relational spaces in which we live,*
*shaping the quality of honoring each other,*
*our livelihoods, and the land.*

*Help me see what you see and sense what you sense.*
*There is so much to notice beyond my own perspective.*
*And let me show you the miracles I see,*
*until the vastness of the world*
*unfolds before us.*

# Listening

*Lean in.*
*Feel the pull of the gravitational field of another.*
*Orbit their sphere with curiosity, wonder,*
*and sacred attention.*

*Lean in.*
*Attune to the pace of breath.*
*Notice the silence between words.*
*I soften my gaze*
*and take in everything.*
*Full presence, here and now.*
*Trust grows in this soil.*

*Lean in.*
*Listen to another's soul.*
*Let the words I hear lead me through their*
*inner caverns of thought, feeling and experience*
*to the fire in the center of their belly*
*and the dreams hidden deep in their heart.*

*Lean in.*
*Follow.*
*I am a guest in someone else's unique world.*
*I clothe myself in humility and curiosity*
*and am led by the gift of another's experience.*
*I receive with grace and gratitude*
*this honor being given.*

*Lean in.*
*Walk the bridge*
*that crosses the gap in understanding.*
*Let empathy and respect dissolve the chasm.*
*Listening is not an act of agreement,*
*it is an act of respect, collaboration and learning.*

*Lean in.*
*We are equals.*
*Your dignity and my dignity are entwined.*
*Hearing what you care about,*
*I see myself mirrored in you.*
*Your cherished needs are as familiar*
*and precious to me as my own.*
*Roots entwined, we grow from the same soil*
*and reach toward the same sun.*

*Lean in if I dare.*
*Listening is a courageous choice,*
*made by those brave enough*
*to be changed by what they hear.*

*Willing to be changed*
*in this process of accompaniment,*
*I become more fully who I am,*
*knowing myself and another*
*more intimately than before.*

*Leaning in,*
*I fall into love.*

INNER PRACTICE #5

# Talking

*Before I speak, may I descend into my bones, my gut, my heart
and reclaim the essence of who I am.
From there, may I rise to meet the world,
offering what I cherish most with honesty and care.*

*May I have the courage to risk being seen and known.
May the words I choose be true to my soul, and the manner
in which I speak be true to my nature and heart.*

*May my vulnerability be raw and unconcealed
so you can feel and see yourself in me.
May I speak passionately without shame, letting what is truly
authentic carve and shape the landscape between us.*

*When disclosing my undefended essence,
may I stay at the pace of my heart,
choosing to slowly peel layers away or to dive straight to the core
in honor of all that is real and alive.*

*May I acknowledge and take responsibility
for what I choose to share and how I choose to say it.
May I be responsive to any and all impact my words
may have on others and reach for repair for any harm.
May kindness and truth be my guide.*

*May I understand the seasons, life cycles and timing
in which my honesty is offered,
so I can discern how my words will best serve.*

*May my words radiate trust in our common humanity,
transforming what seems broken or impossible
into the elegant possibility of connection.*

*May my words call us into action,
with clarity, practicality and love
that inspire new frameworks for living.*

*May my words be invitational,
respecting each response whether "yes" or "no."*

*May my cry for justice be fierce, clear and compassionate.
May my bones unlock the hidden secrets of ancestors
and my words speak that which has yet to be heard.
May my words be free from violence,
yet powerful and swift enough to protect.*

*May I never forget that in this interconnected world
everything I say or do is bound by relationships,
that my words have power to rupture or heal,
to reveal or cloud human dignity.*

*As trees express themselves in blossom and color
may my speech inspire kindness,
soaring high like the song of the black necked crane
yet rooted in soft ground and the fire of the earth.*

# Agency to Act

*Prepare by fully absorbing*
*this moment in which you stand.*
*Notice the land around you,*
*the unique calls of the birds,*
*the direction of the wind,*
*the feel of the soil.*

*Ground your act of creation*
*in solidarity with the land*
*upon which you reside as a guest.*

*Assemble bones, breath, hands and skills*
*alongside dreams and responsibility.*

*Stir.*

*Shape your heart's longings*
*into tangible possibilities and practical forms*
*with attention to details that are doable, positive,*
*specific and accessible now.*

*Sprinkle abundantly with variety.*
*There are many ways to live your values.*
*Hold your needs fiercely and close to your heart,*
*but offer strategies with fluidity and lightness.*

*Bake in the fire of trial and error*
*until risen and softened in the heat.*

*Season with courage to repair the world.*
*What you believe is revealed in what you do.*

*Simmer the sauce of discernment and feedback,*
*always stirring, tasting and adjusting*
*based on what you learn.*

*Finish by lavishly pouring that sauce*
*on the dreams you have*
*shaped and baked.*

*Your life is your message.*
*Present it with grace.*

*Then turn toward one another*
*in joy and gratitude.*

*Serve warm.*

*Savor.*

# *Humility and Learning*

*I cultivate curiosity and openness,*
*remembering my understanding is limited,*
*and there is always more to learn.*

*It's OK to be confused or disturbed.*
*There is inevitably a teacher nearby.*

*Everyone*
*is*
*our*
*teacher.*

*No exceptions.*

*I learn about water by swimming,*
*I learn about sky by flying,*
*I learn about new perspectives by listening,*
*I learn about the web of life by falling into*
*relationship with everything.*

*Savor learning,*
*savor not knowing,*
*savor new ways of seeing.*
*I know that once tasted,*
*there is no turning back.*

*My practice:*
*to greet the miracle of*
*the unknown*
*with open arms.*

*Transformed*
*moment by moment,*
*I can never step into the*
*same river of life twice.*

*I am changed with each breath*
*and each new awareness.*

*Now has newly arrived.*

*Celebrating*
*fresh ways of seeing*
*that emerge*
*in every direction,*
*I open my eyes and see*
*the world continually flowering.*

INNER PRACTICE #8

# Relationship with Power

*When power first came knocking at my door,*
*I was scared and locked the door*
*to keep danger and overwhelm outside.*
*I turned out the lights and hid.*

*Next, I resolved to grab all the power I could,*
*amassing a fortress to protect me*
*thinking I could control danger*
*by being the one in charge.*

*But one day, hands in the soil while planting seeds,*
*I saw power as the birthright of us all;*
*each seed and animal with innate abilities to attend to needs,*
*sharing power through the interplay*
*of giving and receiving.*

*I understood then that power is strongest and safest*
*when there is mutual influence, sharing and collaboration.*

*Now when power comes knocking at the door*
*I invite it in to sit with me by my inner fire.*

*I ask power whom it serves, if it is the kind that*
*repairs harm and restores vitality and hope.*
*I ask why it is calling on me at this crucial hour.*

*If power answers that it is here*
*to serve the well-being of all,*
*I listen intently and embrace its wisdom.*

Power reminds me
that the forces of domination and oppression
are not true power but fear in disguise.

Power reminds me
that responding with submission or rebellion
are not my only alternatives.
That I always have inner choice even
when my options seem limited.

Power reminds me
that the resources I cultivate on the inside
have the strength to move mountains.

When power comes knocking at the door,
I know it's time to discover my courage
and no longer turn away from
my immeasurable strength.

Power calls upon my inner fire
to serve beloved community.
Power calls upon my strength
to stand firmly rooted in dignity and grace.
Power calls upon my heart to work toward equity for all
even when the way forward is unclear.

I nod.
Daunted by this call
but willing to find the support I need in order to say yes,
I raise my eyes toward the dawn,
center my power in the heartbeat of love,
and take my next step.

# *Grieving and Mourning*

*Finding myself alone with Grief,*
*I'm surprised by the unbidden visitor*
*and painfully turn to face a shock unbearable.*

*Walls close in*
*intensifying my pain,*
*stifling breath from my lungs,*
*dreams ripped from their rightful place*
*in my body.*

*Then the door to the room opens quietly.*
*Understanding walks in*
*and starts a fire in the hearth,*
*then tenderly places a chair opposite Grief.*
*Understanding leans in and listens*
*and listens and listens.*

*After awhile, when the room is warmer,*
*Rest arrives,*
*mercifully giving respite from the rawness*
*of rage, confusion and pain.*

*Gratitude surprises all,*
*timing their arrival so unexpectedly.*
*Yet when their chair finds a spot near Grief*
*it is impossible to imagine Gratitude was ever absent.*

When the day breaks, in walks Peace.
Peace often arrives last, waiting for acceptance
and familiarity to grow silently in the unlit corners.
Peace places their chair solidly next to Grief,
extending a hand to say, "We are here together."

Grief and me, now accompanied in a circle of support,
find ourselves between Peace and Gratitude
where we hold each other through the hard nights.

For a moment,
there is nothing to say, nothing to do.
Together we mourn and find comfort in the embrace
of this circle of friends.

Slowly it dawns on me
that our circle of Being
has taken place in
the womb of Life.

I emerge changed,
entering a world that is
different than the one I knew.

I breath in the new life
welcoming all  parts of myself.

INNER PRACTICE #10

# Discernment

*Listening to my heart,*
*I feel into what pulls me toward life*
*and what pushes me away.*

*As my eyes take in the world around me,*
*my mind interprets the meaning of what I'm seeing,*
*deciding if it is aligned with my inner values*
*or smothering that which I cherish.*

*My body rides the waves*
*moving toward needs...*
*moving away from needs...*
*moving toward...*
*moving away...*
*toward...*
*away...*

*Keeping my attention on the fulfillment of needs,*
*I reflect on the complexity, nuances and shades of grey.*

*My internal compass differentiates between*
*judgments based on the honoring of all needs,*
*and the externally learned judgments of*
*who is right and who is wrong.*

*Aligning my head, heart, body and soul*
*I feel into it all*
*and move toward life.*

# *Choice*

*In times when I'm confused and torn,*
*my soul softly whispers,*
*"Never give up*
*your power*
*to respond to life*
*in this moment*
*and the next."*

*I don't always like*
*the options around me.*
*They are too often constrained,*
*limited, dependent on context*
*of the situation and moment.*

*Taking in what lies around me,*
*I meet the outer constraints with an inner resolve*
*to hold onto my agency and freedom.*

*I find my ability to choose deep within,*
*ever present*
*waiting*
*for me*
*to*
*act.*

# *Gratitude*

*Enormous power*
*is unleashed*
*while*

*CELEBRATING*
*LIFE.*

*When the glow of*
*wonder and meaning*
*shine through*
*words or actions,*

*Pause.*

*Offer*
*acknowledgement*
*&*
*thanks.*

*In this moment,*
*we have become*
*what we seek.*

*How joyful it is to be alive.*

## CHAPTER 2

# Systemic Awareness

✣

## Contextual Considerations
## for Dialogue

*We meet at this moment*
*having traveled through different lands*
*and along different paths.*

*I discovered my strength in the mountains.*
*You found your courage on the rivers.*
*They claimed dignity in the depth of the oceans.*
*Others embraced grace in the forests.*

*Here and now,*
*our complicated histories meet,*
*the traditions passed on to us by our ancestors meet,*
*our personal longings and unique life experiences meet.*
*Here and now,*
*the social, economic and cultural opportunities*
*each have been given or denied meet.*

*I read the trees.*
*You read the wind.*
*They read the ice formations.*
*Others read the stars.*

*Sometimes I am the oppressed, sometimes the oppressor.*
*Those roles shifting with circumstance and seasons.*
*Let us name hard truths as we each see them*
*and not turn from our responsibility*
*to find an equitable way forward*
*side by side.*

*I arrive with the exploration of who I am.*
*You arrive with rituals of who you have been.*
*They arrive with dreams of the future.*
*Others arrive clutching the unknown.*
*All of us are cloaked in the complexity*
*of being alive now.*

*As we deepen into dialogue*
*infinite combinations of complexity ebb and flow.*
*Can we see what is missing as well as what is present?*

*Each new revelation and understanding shifts*
*how we are in relation to one another and ourselves.*

*Our awareness of the spaces we inhabit matter*
*as we reach for each other across differences*

*if we are to finally see*

*We are all*
*I, you, they, others.*

# Cultural Diversity

*definition:*
*acknowledging the existence and respecting the presence of*
*a variety of cultural values, lenses, norms, and behaviors*
*within society at local, national and international levels.*
*\*\**


*Our ways of being,*
*passed through generations,*
*tapestries woven of relationships, events and traditions,*
*shape the different ways we see the world.*

*Show me your ways and I will show you mine.*

*What is it you see in the sky or in the space between us?*
*What do you hear in the sound of the waterfall*
*or in the silence that fills the room?*
*What does your body feel in the pounding of the waves*
*or in the reverberation of words spoken*
*in the spaces we inhabit together?*

*If you are willing, speak to me honestly*
*so I may understand.*

*Show me your ways and I will show you mine.*

*I will share if our differences thrill my heart,*
*or pump adrenaline throughout my body in fear.*
*I will reveal rituals and practices that tell me I belong*
*and describe the loneliness when those rituals are not there.*
*I will share how my background has trained me to see*
*certain things that others may not see.*

*If I am willing, I will speak honestly*
*so you may understand.*

*Together may we recognize, celebrate and honor*
*the diversity within our gathering.*

*Together may we navigate our differences*
*and hold our multicultural understandings*
*with humility and curiosity.*

*Show me your ways and I will show you mine.*

*We will be lantern carriers for each other*
*as we journey through this*
*dynamic, multifaceted world.*

# Social Location

*definition:*
*the combination of all social identities*
*to which one belongs.*
*a unique expression of an individual's*
*place in the social fabric*
*⁎⁎*

*All parts of me*
*created from different galaxies,*
*clustering together*
*to form a new celestial being*
*never before assembled*
*in this distinct way.*

*All parts of you*
*created from different star systems,*
*orbiting the sun of your soul*
*until a unique cosmic heaven*
*is given shape and form.*

*All identities are welcome here.*

*Each of us is a remarkably unique constellation
of power, rank, race, gender, skin color,
caste, abilities, sexual orientation,
education, religion, politics, class,
marital status, nationality,
profession, language and
personal history.*

*Time and experiences
bring on-going changes
in this dance of the stars.*

*The gift of each unique vantage point
can help us see the whole
and to breathe in the
wonder and awe
of the
night sky.*

SYSTEMIC AWARENESS #3

# *Trauma*

*definition:*
*overwhelming experiences that leave long-term*
*distressing reverberations on individuals and communities.*
*these experiences can be shocking events,*
*relational-developmental distress or systemic oppression.*
*\*\**

*A loud CRACK splits my world apart.*
*A chasm looms before me, crossing seems impossible.*

*The ground spins, all reliable orientation lost.*
*I stagger, confused and disoriented.*
*The cold polar winds seem to come from the east*
*while what was rooted in the south*
*blows frantically in the west.*

*Chronic exhaustion from the on-going*
*weight of oppression crushes me,*
*the burden of inequitable social systems*
*built on the backs of my people.*

*My inner flame quivers as I wrestle*
*with what I've been fed and have ingested.*

*Events sparked long ago fight to live in the present.*
*Time adrift on waves left by the storm,*
*past and present indistinguishable*
*jumbled together here and now.*

When trust is broken and not repaired,
something breaks deep inside.
With the compass lost at sea, chaos takes the helm.
I rise up and fight for control to make things right again.
When my fevered efforts fail to bring peace,
I drop into the depths of shame and powerlessness.
Wariness becomes my shield and
distance my protector.

None of us escape trauma,
though the kinds and severities we experience differ.

With luck, we somehow find our way
into the healing transformative belly of the dragon
where fires of attunement warm the body,
and understanding stitches pieces
of our life back together again.

Where quiet replaces the cacophony
that previously could not be silenced.
Where healing arises from secure,
trusting relationships,
that mitigate terror and loss.

In the belly of transformation,
We find rituals that re-member
the pieces of ourselves.

We emerge with scars and memories,
yet wiser and more resilient
than ever before.

# *Bias and Implicit Bias*

*definition:*
*bias: an internal inclination or tendency*
*toward or against something or someone.*
*implicit bias: unconscious internal attitudes and stereotypes*
*about individuals or groups.*
*\*\**

*I am wired*
*to be enlivened by difference*
*alert to the smallest nuance*
*that shouts, "Stranger!"*

*Internally trusting what is familiar*
*and shying away from what is new,*
*I ping-pong my way back and forth*
*between comfort and discomfort.*

*Beware!*

*Having learned to fear some faces*
*and welcome others,*
*my unconscious reactions*
*can lead to unintended harm*
*or unintended favor.*

*With compassionate self-knowing*
*I patiently rewire internal tendencies I have toward others*
*learning to recognize the inherent dignity of all.*

# *Prejudice*

*definition:*
*preconceived opinions, beliefs or attitudes in one's head*
*that are unsupported by reason and/or based on*
*limited information or experience*
*about groups of people or cultural practices.*
**

*I have an internal picture of you,*
*two dimensional, simple bold lines and grayscale tones,*
*drawn by cultural messages that I have made my own.*

*I keep you colored between the lines*
*no room for spilling over*
*or blurring what contains you.*

*I know who you are.*
*I know what you think.*
*I know your intentions.*
*I know your place.*

*or do I?*

*Perhaps if I look away from my*
*prefabricated image for just a moment,*
*you will walk off the page and touch me on the shoulder.*

*I'll turn and see your aliveness,*
*wondering how my flat image with bold lines*
*could ever have seemed real.*

# Discrimination

*definition:*
*negative actions or inappropriate treatment*
*toward individuals or groups*
*based on their perceived group membership.*
*✳✳*

*As I slowly become aware of what I am doing,*
*I watch in horror as my prejudice*
*finds pathways to move from my mental attitudes*
*out through my fingers, hands, feet, voice.*

*I watch the violence of my actions*
*wound what is sacred.*

*I watch the hurtful impact of my words*
*destroy any hope of trust between us.*

*This harm isn't dispersed equally.*
*I inflict suffering on those*
*I've learned to categorize and hate.*

*It's gut wrenching to watch my own inhumanity.*

*I take responsibility,*
*and like this poem,*
*search for a way*
*to make it end.*

SYSTEMIC AWARENESS #7

# Rank

*definition:*
*position in a social hierarchy.*
**

*As we enter the room*
*we start to place each other*
*on rungs of a ladder*
*according to relative social value*
*we each possess:*

*class*
*caste*
*position*
*wealth*
*status*
*power*
*education*
*religion*
*race*
*ethnicity*
*gender*
*sexual orientation*
*marital status*

*My social status depends on*
*who else is in the room*
*and the purpose of our gathering.*

*My classification is informed at birth*
*inherited from my ancestors,*
*placing me high or low*
*without agency on my part.*

*My placement is cultivated through*
*education, practice and learning,*
*earned through contribution*
*and applied knowledge*
*that impact the group.*

*My rank determines my access to resources*
*and the degree of freedom I have*
*to choose my own way and benefit from the*
*consequences of my choices.*

*My position carries responsibility and expectations*
*through the roles, duties and lifestyle*
*I take on.*

*Has anyone ever thought*
*of laying this social ladder*
*flat on the floor?*

# *Privilege*

*definition:*
*access to resources, social advantages or benefits simply by*
*belonging to certain social identity groups without requiring*
*any action or awareness on the part of the individual.*
\*\*

*I emerge from the womb*
*identified by society, not because of who I am,*
*but according to whom I belong.*

*I find ease in being part of a group*
*when it gives me access to the social resources*
*allotted to that particular group.*

*I also experience mourning,*
*when my membership with that same group—*
*in other settings—*
*denies me access to social benefits and advantages*
*that would help me thrive.*

*Seeking self-responsibility, I pause and look around.*

*Do I have privilege in this moment?*
*Am I using it to build inclusive community?*
*Am I using it to center those with less privilege?*
*Am I using it to turn good intentions into beneficial impact?*

*We do not choose our level of privilege.*
*It is how we use it that defines our character.*

# Structural Power

*definition:*
*access to external resources and decision making ability*
*within a system because of one's title, role, or social status.*
*\*\**

*The ways we are organized have both*
*explicit authorized forms and implicit subjective shadows.*
*I watch the way power moves between shadow and form,*
*casting light on our relationships and roles as we gather.*

*Who in this setting has the most capacity to*
*mobilize resources to attend to needs?*

*Who gets to make which decisions?*

*Who has the ability to determine consequences,*
*to influence and affect negatively or positively*
*another person or group?*

*Who is being served most by power?*

*To whom is power given through*
*trust and respect for expertise?*
*To whom is power given through fear?*

*From whom has power been taken*
*due to prejudice or distrust?*
*Where is power imposed structurally in violent ways*
*that put groups or individuals in harm's way?*

*These questions bring into view the shadow and the light.*

*When I am in a power-down position*
*I may be tempted to submit or rebel.*
*Instead, I remember to hold onto my inner power*
*to choose my response in any situation*
*even if I don't like my options.*

*When I have less formal power than others,*
*my vantage point can unveil what is hidden in plain sight*
*to those entrusted with power.*
*I remember that I can choose whether or not to engage*
*in dialogue that may come at a cost to my well-being.*

*When I am in a power-up position,*
*I may have less capacity to see the effects of my actions.*
*Privilege protects me from having to feel the impacts*
*my choices have on others.*

*I respect the choices of those with less power*
*to decide if, when, and how to engage with me.*
*Honest dialogue requires mutuality and trust.*

*Aware of individual and collective trauma*
*resulting from power used to oppress,*
*I take responsibility to listen more and talk less,*
*guided by the wisdom and leadership*
*of those impacted most directly by my choices.*

*I am committed to fully using all power entrusted to me*
*for collective healing, collective well-being,*
*and collective joy.*

# Isms

*definition:*
*a socially constructed ideology, theory or doctrine.*
*a system or practice of advantage or oppression*
*based on target identity.*
*\*\**

*We build complicated towers,*
*socially constructed palaces of power.*

*We claim they are natural*
*like rivers flowing to the sea*
*or leaves falling from trees.*

*Racism*
*Colorism*
*Ableism*
*Ageism*
*Classism*
*Sexism*
*Heterosexism*
*Ethnocentrism*
*Anthropocentrism*

*Yet in time, these towers and illusions crumble*
*as darkness gives way to dawn and*
*winter melts into spring.*

# *Intersectionality*

*definition:*
*the overlapping of social categorizations (such as race, class,*
*and gender) that result in mutually linked systems that*
*compound discrimination, disadvantage and/or oppression.*
*an acknowledgment that each person has their*
*own unique experience of inequality.*
*(term coined by Kimberly Crenshaw)*
\*\*

*From birth,*
*the world has chosen for me*
*the burdens I must bear*
*because of who I am.*

*Born female in a patriarchal world,*
*black in a dominantly white culture,*
*poor in a capitalist class system.*

*Any one of these is hard to carry.*
*Yet combined,*
*the intensified pressure unjustly stresses*
*my overburdened body.*

*You struggle, too, with your own*
*accumulation of systemic weights,*
*piled like boulder upon boulder,*
*precariously balanced as you make your way*
*through your configuration of oppression.*

*These intersections matter*
*if we want to see each other fully*
*and work toward sharing the load equally.*

*Let us name the places that hurt,*
*the burdens that are heavy,*
*the suffering we endure.*

*Maybe in the naming*
*we will see each other more.*
*Maybe in the seeing*
*we will understand each other more.*
*Maybe in the understanding*
*we will love each other more.*
*Maybe in the loving*
*we will undo the systems that burden us*
*and dance for the first time*
*equal and free.*

## CHAPTER 3

# Dialogue in Action

❧

## I. What is Dialogue?

*When two or more gather and eyes meet,*
*meaningful conversation summons us.*
*For thousands of years the heat of fire and beauty of stars*
*called forth stories, songs, resonant companionship*
*and innovative ideas.*

*The womb of the earth provides*
*nurturing conditions for life to emerge.*
*Each birth different depending on the seeds and seasons.*

*So it is with authentic dialogue.*
*It is the womb that nurtures*
*the unfolding relationship between us,*
*the container out of which new configurations,*
*collaborations and possibilities emerge.*

*Each dialogue is unique,*
*structured not to restrict or control,*
*but to allow emergence and flow.*
*A rising tide that lifts all boats.*

*Dialogue happens in the sphere of equals.*
*Roles, rank, privilege, and power give way to*
*omnidirectional listening and speaking*
*where each person speaks freely and is deeply heard.*

*Keeping our collective gaze on our purpose
we balance who is centered and when,
attending throughout the labor to the
equitable emergence of perspectives.*

*We move through mutual understanding,
self-responsibility, action, and review.
All stages take the time they take.*

*Dialogue's rhythm and direction
flows like a river, adapting
as the force of water requires,
guided by the banks of what we value
to which we return again and again.*

*Authentic dialogue invites courageous risk,
revealing what is vulnerable and true,
willing to hear, believe, and be changed
by what we encounter.*

*We are inextricably in this together
and what we sow between us
is what we harvest
to get us through the winter.*

*Listen, speak, act,
create with love
so together
we may call in the dawn.*

# II.  The Art of Dialogue

*The space between us*
*is where worlds are created and destroyed,*
*the unknown in which all possibility lies.*

*Each of us arrives in this space*
*carrying cultures, experiences, and traditions*
*in our bones.*

*Each if us arrives in this space*
*with perspective that only our eyes see,*
*a perspective that's essential to the whole.*

*Let us be weavers of possibilities.*
*Let us talk honestly, revealing what we care about.*
*Let us voice our dreams and name our hurts.*
*Let us listen to each other as if each word holds*
*the key to our redemption.*

*Let us be weavers of relationships,*
*one thread, one resonant word,*
*one compassionate action at a time.*
*Threading back and forth what we deem essential,*
*giving and receiving respect and joy,*
*aware that our needs are*
*interconnected and inseparable.*

*Let us be weavers of community,*
*fashioned by multicolored threads from around the world,*
*interlacing prismatic intricacy into dynamic designs*
*that tell stories of who we are collectively.*
*Each thread with a place and purpose.*

*Let us be weavers of power,*
*where leaders follow and followers lead,*
*open to the wisdom and influence of all,*
*cultivating resources that serve the whole.*

*Let us be weavers of the future.*
*Back and forth with our speaking and listening,*
*designing patterns to sustain the next generation.*

*Elevate the quality of our dialogue*
*for it determines the quality of our lives.*
*Let us weave fabric of beauty, durability and warmth*
*that will enfold all children.*

*Dialogue arises from the same faith that parts seas,*
*moves mountains, and heals the sick.*
*Dialogue makes it possible to feed the hungry,*
*provide shelter and safety, turn enemies into friends,*
*and unleash the transformative fire of love.*

*As we deeply listen*
*to what is emerging in the space between us,*
*we become weavers of miracles.*

# Shared and Clear Purpose

*We have come here for a reason*
*the clarity of which determines our process*
*and level of satisfaction with the outcome.*

*Purpose comes in a myriad of forms:*
*maybe a task to do,*
*a decision to make,*
*a crises to respond to,*
*a new project to brainstorm.*

*Perhaps*
*to increase understanding,*
*repair relationships,*
*explore process,*
*celebrate,*
*mourn.*

*Take a moment*
*to source purpose*
*from life's deep well.*

*What is being asked of us now*
*to move us toward*
*wholeness?*

# Focus on Connection

*There's a quality of connection within which*
*what was invisible is seen,*
*what was despised is redeemed,*
*what was separate is returned to the whole,*
*and what was lost is found.*

*That is the connection we seek here.*
*Walls crumble and obstacles disperse*
*in the presence of such grace.*

*Curiosity and care are the*
*building blocks of connection.*
*When I stand in your shoes,*
*the world you see makes sense to me*
*and our common humanity unmistakable.*

*Here we seek genuine relationship*
*not transactional bartering.*
*A place where soil and seed*
*live in harmony with sun and rain.*

*With every perspective honored and included,*
*no one gives up or gives in.*
*Trust, reciprocity and consideration*
*breed agreements of stability and durability.*

*Presence and empathic listening*
*create understanding and goodwill*
*out of which effective choices arise.*

*Create the quality of connection that honors*
*all needs equally and attends to them*
*through natural giving.*
*That leads to an abundant harvest.*

*So let connection be our focus,*
*trusting that all that is needed will*
*flow from the wellspring of who we are*
*as naturally as a river finds its way to the sea.*

# Finding Common Ground

*Though we stand on different continents,*
*we see the same moon.*
*Though we climb different trees,*
*we are part of the same forest.*
*Though we choose different strategies*
*we seek the same qualities of life.*

*The love of family,*
*the satisfaction of food,*
*the relief from pain,*
*the solace of safety.*

*We all need these to thrive:*
*Health, choice, meaning, purpose,*
*connection, friendship, water, air,*
*learning, beauty, celebration, mourning,*
*honest expression, empathy, clarity, freedom,*
*empowerment, acceptance, integrity,*
*peace and love.*
*All are common ground.*

*Hidden within our words and actions,*
*buried in the common ground of our needs,*
*are the dreams we share*
*waiting for light and warmth*
*to sprout new wings.*

# Cultivating Trust

Trust begins to grow the moment
I convey to you that I hold your needs
as precious to me as my own.

Trust between us grows steadfast
as acceptance gains access to our hearts.
We turn toward each other with curiosity and humility.

I seek out alignment between what you say and do.
You challenge if I "walk my talk."
Those first steps to trust are so important.
Keep going, mature trust grows
with time and experience.
Trust is a choice we make again and again.

Like the caterpillar in the cocoon,
our sense of trust liquifies as paradox
and complexity spin around us.

Transformed by experience,
trust between us emerges bravely,
with faith in one's ability to face whatever arises,
committed to the acceptance of what is.

Trust no longer lies in predictability,
but in our choice to navigate truth
with respect and empathy,
to learn and emerge together whole.

DIALOGUE PRACTICE #5
# *Creating Time to Recenter*

*When I get knocked off balance*
*and need to find my footing again,*
*I turn inward to the place beyond thought*
*and remember my essential nature.*

*I feel into my body,*
*listen to my heart,*
*observe my mind,*
*ground in purpose.*

*I am committed to dissolving my defenses,*
*to risking exposure of my true self.*
*My defenses only hide and constrain*
*what is intrinsically indestructible.*
*Touching my essence I discover*
*I am awake, alive and strong.*

*Always with me,*
*I find dignity and compassion*
*in my inner sanctuary.*
*I return again and again to this*
*refuge to gather clarity and strength.*

*Then, like an orca breaching,*
*I rise from my inner depths*
*and offer myself fully into the*
*widening circles of this mysterious world.*

# *Consent*

When we both freely choose to be here
with awareness of consequences,
we begin to dialogue as equals.

Consent is an on-going conversation,
potentially changing with time and circumstance.
The option of saying no is always available.
Inquiring regularly, we confirm whether or not
our agreement to continue still stands.

Consent requires the absence
of duress, coercion and fear.

Knowledgeable, positive consent requires
ability, specificity, and honesty.
Questions are invited and welcome.

Expressed consent,
clearly and freely communicated
with affirmative, voluntary words or willful actions
is foundational to trust and
essential for building healthy,
respectful, and safe relationships.

# Naming Power Dynamics

*When the elephant is in the room,*
*acknowledge and name it.*
*It will appreciate the welcome*
*and stop trampling on people.*

*It doesn't go away*
*it just finds its place*
*while we rearrange ourselves*
*so we all can see each other*
*and work together in the configuration*
*we find ourselves in.*

*Each of our vantage points sheds different light*
*on constraints, challenges, and opportunities.*

*Together we discover*
*who is entrusted with which decisions.*

*With the elephant named,*
*we can move with clarity*
*since "what is"*
*has become visible to all.*

*There is power in naming.*
*Our nervous systems settle.*
*We arrive at choice.*

*And the elephant takes a place at the table.*

# *Tracking*

*Foxes leave tracks in the snow*
*showing where they've been*
*and the direction they are headed.*

*Dialogue leaves tracks*
*of who has been heard,*
*whose needs are on the table,*
*what requests have been tended to,*
*what strategies offered.*

*Foxes hunt by aligning the sound of prey*
*with earth's magnetic fields.*
*Direct, prescribed lines don't always yield a meal.*
*Coming into sync calls for flexibility and fluidity.*

*In dialogue we seek alignment*
*between needs, strategies, resources, access.*
*We roam flexibly in and out of ways of knowing*
*until we see each other clearly.*

*We track messages spoken*
*through expressions, words and silence.*
*Imprints left in all directions, each voice important*
*to find our shared way to the felt center of our purpose.*

*We follow internalized songs of the earth*
*until we arrive in a field of mutual understanding.*
*Our tools for this journey:*
*Truth telling, deep listening, confirmation that*
*message sent is message received.*

*Grounded in mutual understanding,*
*we search for the path of self-responsibility.*
*Each person recognizing*
*how their choices impact the whole.*

*Carrying our purpose onward,*
*we find our way into action,*
*matching resources with needs,*
*matching requests with offers,*
*giving tangible form to dreams.*

*Before leaving, turn*
*and take in the full vista of the journey.*
*Look out over the glistening snow*
*to see how far we have come*
*and bless what will unfold next.*

*By listening to body, heart and mind,*
*consider whether the decisions we made*
*honor and satisfy the hopes we were trying to achieve.*
*If so, celebrate. If not, adjust.*

*If you get momentarily lost, pause.*
*The path will find you if you but listen.*

*When dialogue gets hard,*
*do not curse the storm for it brings the snow*
*where our tracks can be clearly seen*
*and our hearts can find the way.*

# Passing Back and Forth

*Bees gather pollen*
*from all the flowers in the field*
*taking it to the central hive*
*where the collection is*
*transformed into honey.*

*No single flower provides all the pollen*
*No single bee collects all the food.*
*Bees guide each other to sweetness by dancing,*
*ensuring the best harvest to benefit the whole.*

*In authentic dialogue*
*each person's ideas, feelings, dreams*
*are part of the harvest needed for*
*collective honey to be made.*

*Gather meaning by inviting all to speak.*
*Back and forth the speaking is passed,*
*back and forth the listening is carried.*

*Dialogue is an exchange,*
*swaying rhythmically between perspectives,*
*collecting the sweet wisdom of all,*
*then blending into honey*
*our shared hopes and dreams.*

# *Checking In*

*When assumptions frame
the way we see each other,
pause. Check it out.*

*When we have a guess
about what it is like
to stand in another's shoes,
pause. Check it out.*

*When we think we understand
the meaning being made
of any word, look, action or event,
pause. Check it out.*

*We cannot absolutely know another's experience.
Our own understanding is too uniquely limited
to grasp the whole universe another inhabits.*

*We can, however, check in with one another to see if
our assumptions, understandings, guesses,
feelings and perspectives
resonate or match
another's life experience.*

*Checking in, we see more clearly and accurately
the way the world looks through each other's eyes.
Pause and savor the feast of possibilities.*

# *Repair*

When cold winds of aggression blow in from the north
and words turn to ice as they are spoken,
it's time to shore up the shelter of care that
keeps us safe and warm.

Outside the branches are weighed down
by wet snow accumulated bit by bit over time.
The slightest wind could break the branch.

Yet that same wind, if gentle and timely enough,
could blow the snow from the branch
to release the burden and free the limb.

So it is when our words burden each other
and sharp cold barbs pierce the heart.
Let the winds of repair be gentle and timely
addressing harm before the weight is overbearing.

The burden may come in the form of distrust:
Suggestions of not fitting in
or words that imply one's home is elsewhere.

Listen to the pain and fatigue
of those who carry the burden.
Acknowledge that the words of this moment
may only be the latest snowflake in a
lifetime of stormy winds and freezing conditions,
yet they continue the on-going historical
onslaught of harm.

When icy words fall from your own lips,
do not turn away, but acknowledge and feel the cold.
Allow it to cut through your skin until you, too,
can know the pain you unknowingly inflict
and mourn the ramifications.

Listen to those impacted and
learn about the fullness of the storm.
Then you will understand that you can choose
to provide refuge rather than amass harm.

If asked, let your expression come from a broken open heart
that assumes full responsibility for your words,
feelings, actions, thoughts, and choices.

The snow will continue to fall on the branches.
We will step on each other's toes.

When that extra weight threatens to break
the integrity of the whole structure,
may we generate warm winds of repair,
restorative and timely enough to free
the entire tree of the burden it carries.

In so doing, discover that our shelter of care
has become a safe space for all.

# Action Plan Requests & Offers

*We have listened to the lessons*
*from the North, South, East and West*
*and crafted a vision of where we want to go.*

*Now we prepare for the actual journey.*

*We gather our resources,*
*inventory individual talents and skills,*
*source the wisdom of past travelers,*
*then assemble what we need to*
*secure safe passage for all.*

*Some will lead, others will follow.*
*Some know how to build shelter,*
*others know how to build trust.*
*Some gather food,*
*others know the ways of fire.*

*Each asks for what they need.*
*Each offers gifts and skills to aid others.*
*In this way, responsibility is shared*
*and our interdependence ensures*
*the well-being of all.*

*We step out carefully on this rocky path*
*as we begin our journey.*
*Every detail matters*
*to make our dreams come into form.*

We source our choices directly from what is essential to life,
root them in compassionate giving from the heart,
build them from available resources.

Each step is specific and concrete,
guided by positive, doable action,
unfolding in the present moment
and willingly given.

At the end of the day we measure how far we've come.

Did our actions achieve what we were hoping for?
Are we closer to the horizon we are heading toward?
Are there new obstacles that require new forms of action?
Do some of our actions need adjustment?
Is there celebration in the progress we have made?

As snow geese gracefully adapt as they fly
with common purpose and direction,
we, too, adjust as we go.

We meet the triumphs and challenges
of our journey with clear requests and offers,
providing sure footing as we
move toward the dawn.

# *Giving and Receiving Feedback*

*Feedback is a gift.*

*It is the offering of one's experience,*
*a present of perspective about what matters,*
*the celebration and mourning of overlapping lives.*

*The purpose? To move and grow in tandem,*
*to journey through authentic expression and receiving*
*arriving at the place of knowing each other more fully,*
*enlivened by learning, mutual understanding*
*and collaboration.*

*Offer feedback with humility and receive it with gratitude.*
*There is vulnerability in both the giving and receiving.*

*Gifts come in a variety of packaging.*
*No matter the wrapping, savor each layer*
*of unveiling to discover all hidden gems.*

*When giving the gift of your perspective,*
*place the treasure of your experience simply inside,*
*unobstructed by excess packaging.*
*Offer with specifics and concrete observations*
*to ground your celebrations and mournings*
*in time and space.*

*Wrap with awareness of our interdependence and equality,*
*as well as our rank, status and power differences.*
*Finish liberally with ribbons of intention*
*for learning and support.*

*Offer your gift with self-responsibility and vulnerability.*
*Check in to learn how your gift is being received.*

*When receiving another's gift of perspective,*
*assume before opening that the gift contains value,*
*even if the packaging is ripped and torn from the journey.*
*Remember you are being gifted with another's experience*
*that can be used as an opportunity to learn and grow.*

*Listen with awareness of our interdependence and equality,*
*as well as our rank, status and power differences.*
*Take self-responsibility for how you hear messages.*
*Check in to see if you've received the full meaning*
*of the present.*

*Find the time and support required to fully understand*
*the feelings and needs of both the giver and receiver.*
*Then decide what to do with the gift. It is your choice.*

*Gifts are exchanged within the context of*
*cultural messages and systems of domination we live in.*
*Bring compassion to any lasting impact of prior feedback.*
*Choose now your own new relationship with these gifts*
*and consider your willingness to consent.*

*We all need confirmation*
*of whether or not*
*we have served life.*

*Feedback is that sacred gift.*

# *Expressing Gratitude*

*When joy stops you in your tracks,*
*do not rush to hurry on.*

*This moment is for celebrating.*
*What one values*
*is tangible here and now.*

*Pause to notice the gentle breeze that cools,*
*or the warmth of the rock under your hand.*
*Feel the ache of your longing*
*give way to the ecstasy of its fulfillment.*

*When what is essential*
*is gifted through another,*
*take the time to say, "Thanks."*

*We can be mirrors for each other's*
*ability to make life wonderful.*
*We can share the joy of contributing to life.*

*Gratitude is acknowledgment and celebration.*
*It is not praise with an agenda to buy love or gain reward.*
*It is not a strategy to escape punishment.*

*It is standing in awe,*
*paying tribute to that which*
*makes life worth living.*

# Epilogue

*My face lights up as you enter the room.*

*You reach out*
*and clasp my hand.*

*Together,*
*we welcome the dawn.*

# Discussion and Journaling Questions

These questions are offered as starting points for personal or group reflection of how concepts in this book might support dialogue, relationships and collaboration.

## Suggestions for engaging with the questions:

Choose to work with 1-2 questions in each chapter that call your attention on any given day or session.

Remember they are just starting points.
Follow your heart and curiosity where you are led.

Putting ideas into practice and cultivating new skills is a process. Be compassionate with yourself and others.

## CHAPTER 1: INNER RESOURCES

*1. What is your "new dawn"? How would you describe the world you want to leave to the next 7 generations?*

*2. Which of the inner practices in Chapter 1 do you consider strengths of yours?*

*3. Which of the inner practices in Chapter 1 would you like to cultivate more fully?*

*4. Are there specific ideas in Chapter 1 that seemed to resonate with your own experience? If so, which ones?*

*5. Are there specific ideas in chapter 1 that are different from your own experience? If so, which ones?*

*6. Do you have people in your life that seem to embody these daily wisdom practices? Who are they and how have conversations with them impacted you?*

*7. Are there situations where you find it easy to live these practices in relationships? What are they?*

*8. Are there situations where you find it challenging to live these practices in relationships? What are they?*

## CHAPTER 2: SYSTEMIC AWARENESS

*1. What is your own social location (your unique combination of social identities) and how does the intersection of your identities affect your life?*

*2. Which "isms" in your immediate social structures impact you the most based on your intersectionality? How do you respond to them as an individual?*

*3. Were there times in your life when your internal bias/ prejudice became external discrimination? How did you feel about that? How do you respond in similar situations now?*

*4. How do you experience prejudice or discrimination in your family and/or community organizations (either acknowledged or not acknowledged)?*

*5. Are there specific ideas in chapter 2 that resonate with your own experience? If so, which ones?*

*6. Are there specific ideas in chapter 2 that are different from your own experience? If so, which ones?*

*7. How can you use your awareness of the topics in Chapter 2 to make conversations in your life more productive, equitable or trusting?*

# CHAPTER 3: DIALOGUE IN ACTION

*1. Are there specific ideas in chapter 3 that resonate with your own experience? If so, which ones?*

*2. Are there specific ideas in chapter 3 that are different from your own experience? If so, which ones?*

*3. Which of these practices is a strength/gift that you consistently bring to dialogues you are involved in?*

*4. Which of these practices do you want to cultivate more fully to use in your conversations?*

*5. Which of these practices do you experience used the most and/or the least in dialogues you are in?*

*6. Which of these practices, if brought into a difficult conversation you are currently experiencing, do you imagine would beneficially shift that conversation?*

*7. Are you surprised by any of these topics named as "dialogue practices"? What other dialogue practices can you think of?*

*8. How do you currently cultivate and/or maintain trust in your relationships? What have you done for repair when trust was broken?*

# Benediction

*Go forth and breathe life into the world.*

*Call in the new dawn.*

*Build Vibrant Peace.*
*Here. Now.*
*Everywhere*
*With Everyone.*

*May joy and gratitude sustain you.*

*May the tracks you leave*
*lead to Beloved Community.*

*May what you say and do be a*
*blessing for future generations.*

# Acknowledgements

*to Mahatma Gandhi, Martin Luther King Jr.,*
*Nelson Mandela and all those who practice nonviolence,*
*for the tools and principles to shape our future*
*into a world that works for all.*

*to Marshall B. Rosenberg,*
*for the gift of Nonviolent Communication*
*and your trust in me.*

*to Jared Finkelstein and Robert Krzisnik*
*for your sacred companionship*
*on this path of nonviolence and dialogue.*
*May your memories be a blessing.*

*to the multitude of teachers, writers, artists*
*whose words and art change my world everyday.*

*to my beloved Bob Salt*
*who believes I have something*
*meaningful to say, and reminds me daily that*
*the power of love is our true power.*

# About the Author

Kathleen Macferran

Holds a vision for a peaceful, thriving, sustainable world.

A world where
peace replaces violence,
love replaces hate,
equity replaces inequity.

Student of Life

Certified Trainer for the
Center for Nonviolent Communication

Former music conductor and public school teacher
www.StrengthofConnection.com

*Choice: A Field Guide for Navigating the Polarization of Our World and Living Interdependently*
(co-authored with Jared Finkelstein)

*How Giraffes Found Their Hearts*
(illustrated by Kenneth Schrag)

*How Giraffes Got Their Ears*
(illustrated by Kenneth Schrag)